THE YUCKY REPTILE ALPHABET BOOK

by Jerry Pallotta
Illustrated by Ralph Masiello

Books by Jerry Pallotta

The Icky Bug Alphabet Book, The Bird Alphabet Book, The Ocean Alphabet Book, The Flower Alphabet Book, The Yucky Reptile Alphabet Book, The Frog Alphabet Book, The Furry Alphabet Book, The Dinosaur Alphabet Book, The Underwater Alphabet Book, The Victory Garden Alphabet Book, The Make Your Own Alphabet Book, Going Lobstering, The Icky Bug Counting Book, Cuenta los insectos

Special thanks to Peter Ranney of Terrapin Station.
. . . Linda, thank you for being a wonderful mother.

Published by Charlesbridge Publishing, 85 Main Street, Watertown, MA 02172 • (617) 926-0329

Library of Congress Cataloging-in-Publication Data

Pallotta, Jerry.
  The yucky reptile alphabet book / by Jerry Pallotta; Ralph Masiello, illustrator.
      p.   cm.
  Summary: Introduces the letters of the alphabet by describing a reptile for each letter, from the armadillo lizard to the dinosaurs of a zillion years ago.
  ISBN 0-88106-680-X (library reinforced)
  ISBN 0-88106-460-2 (trade hardcover)   ISBN 0-88106-454-8 (softcover)
  1. Reptiles–Juvenile literature.   2. English language–Alphabet–Juvenile literature.   [1. Reptiles. 2. Alphabet.]   I. Masiello, Ralph, ill.   II. Title.
QL644.2.P35   1991   89-60425
597.9 — dc20   CIP
Printed in the United States of America   AC
(sc)   10   9   8
(hc)   10   9   8   7   6   5   4   3
(lb)   10   9   8   7   6   5   4   3   2   1

Printed on Recycled Paper.

A a

A is for Armadillo Lizard. When attacked or frightened, the Armadillo Lizard pretends it is a pinecone. It sticks its tail in its mouth and rolls itself into a ball.

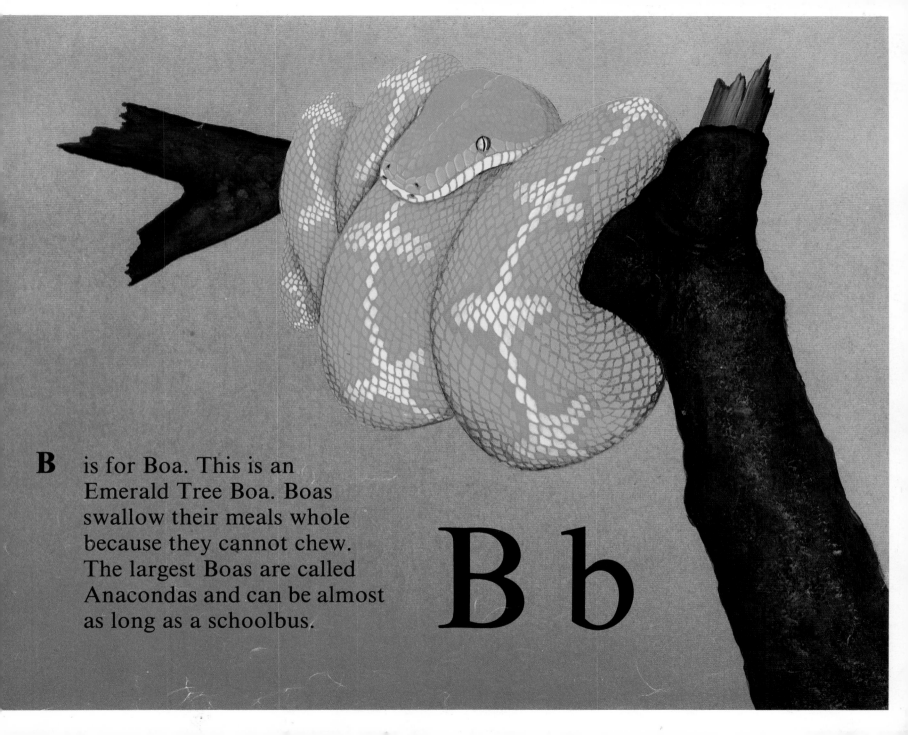

B is for Boa. This is an Emerald Tree Boa. Boas swallow their meals whole because they cannot chew. The largest Boas are called Anacondas and can be almost as long as a schoolbus.

B b

Cc

C is for Chameleon. Chameleons can change color and make their skin match their surroundings. What is most amazing, though, is the Chameleon's incredibly long tongue.

Wow! It really is long! The Chameleon's tongue can be almost twice as long as its body.

Its tongue is perfect for catching insects.

D d

D is for Diamondback Terrapin. Terrapins are turtles. The Diamondback Terrapin has markings on its back that remind some people of diamonds.

Ee

E is for Egg. These are Crocodile Eggs. Birds are not the only creatures that hatch from eggs. Most, but not all, reptiles are born this way.

F is for Frilled Lizard. This Australian lizard pops up its collar and hisses when it wants to scare someone. It can also run very fast on its hind legs.

Ff

G is for Gila Monster. The Gila Monster lives in the desert. It often has a fat tail. The Gila Monster stores food in its tail for times when it cannot find enough to eat or drink.

Gg

H h

H is for Horned Toad. This reptile is not a toad. Since it is round and has such a short tail, people forget that it is a Horned Lizard. When Horned Lizards get mad, they squirt blood out of their eyes.

I i

I is for Iguana. These spooky looking reptiles are sometimes movie stars. When moviemakers take pictures of Iguanas up close, the Iguanas look just like gigantic dinosaurs.

J is for Joint Snake. Joint Snakes are also called Glass Snakes. They are able to break off sections of their tails. Joint Snakes are not really snakes. They are legless lizards.

J j

K k

K is for Knob-tailed Gecko. This reptile never blinks because it cannot move its eyelids. It licks its eyes to keep them clean. Maybe the Knob-tailed Gecko could use a pair of windshield wipers.

The word knob begins with the silent letter k. Let's find a reptile whose name starts with the hard k sound.

K k

K is for Komodo Dragon. The Komodo Dragon is the biggest lizard in the whole world. It is larger and longer than most people.

L is for Leatherback Turtle. This ocean turtle is the largest of all turtles. It is also the most widely travelled of all reptiles. The Leatherback Turtle can be found all over the world in both warm waters and cold waters.

L l

M is for Moloch. Some people call this a Mountain Devil and some people call it a Thorny Devil. It would be hard to keep as a pet because it eats hundreds and hundreds of ants every day.

M m

N n

N is for Night Snake. Night Snakes are nocturnal. This means they do not usually come out during the day. They are ready to come out as soon as the sun goes down.

O o

O   is for Ornate Box Turtle. Box
turtles have a hinged bottom
shell which they can completely
shut to protect their bodies.
The Ornate Box Turtle is
prettier than other
box turtles.

P p **P** is for Pipe Snake. The Pipe Snake has a neat way to fool other animals. It hides its head under its coiled body and lifts up its tail. The end of its tail looks like its head.

Q q

Q is for Queensnake. The Queensnake is a water snake that may have gotten its name because it is a picky eater and likes fancy food. It prefers to eat only soft-shelled crayfish.

R is for Rattlesnake. These snakes make rattle noises by shaking the end of their tails. Not many people like to play with Rattlesnakes because they have poisonous fangs in their mouths.

R r

S is for Skink. Everyone has heard of a skunk but how many people have heard of a Skink? On this page is a Blue-tongued Skink. It did not get its blue tongue from licking blue lollipops. It was born this way.

S s

T t

T is for Tuatara. Tuataras were alive when dinosaurs still roamed the earth. They are different than all other living reptiles although they look like lizards.

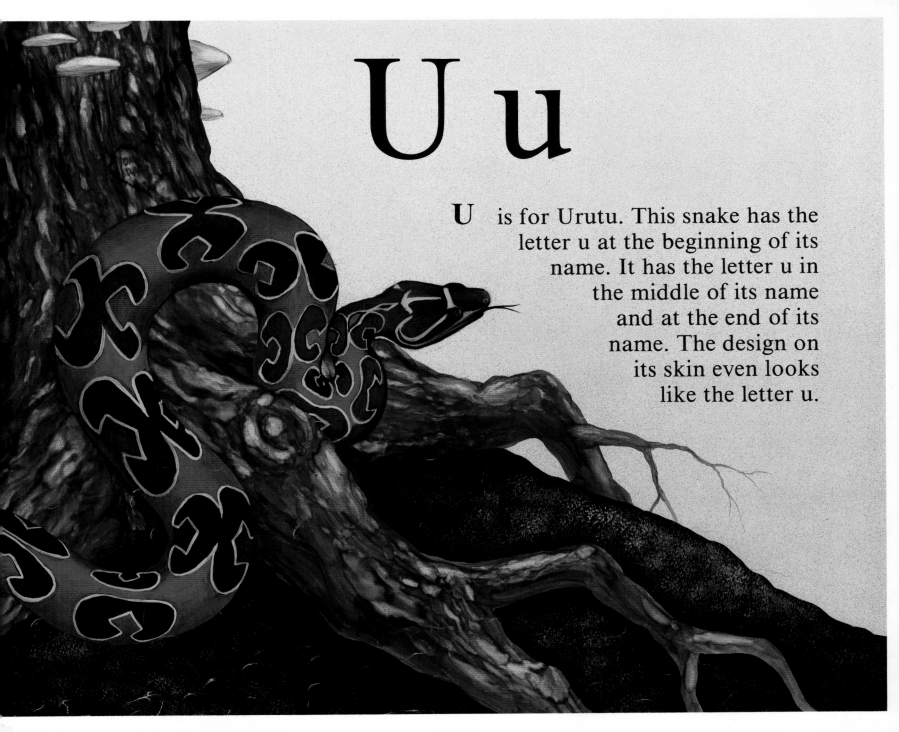

U u

U is for Urutu. This snake has the letter u at the beginning of its name. It has the letter u in the middle of its name and at the end of its name. The design on its skin even looks like the letter u.

V v

V is for Vine Snake.
The Vine Snake is long and thin.
It looks like a skinny piece of
green rope with a head attached.
How can it remember where the end
of its tail is?

W is for Whiptail. In some places almost all of the Whiptails are female. When picked up, Whiptails wiggle their heads from side to side.

X x **X** is for *Xantusia riversiana*. What? What kind of a name is that? This scientific name is much too difficult for young children. People usually call it an Island Night Lizard.

Y y

Y is for Yellow-headed Gecko. Some Geckos have suction cups on their feet that allow them to climb steep, smooth walls. This Yellow-headed Gecko is cute but maybe it would rather be red-headed, orange-headed or purple-headed.

Z z

Z is for Zillions. Zillions of years ago, giant reptiles lived on earth.

The giant reptiles were dinosaurs, but that is another story for another day.

Adults would probably like to know that there are four different living orders of reptiles.

1. *Crocodylia:* Crocodiles, Alligators, Caimans and Gavials
2. *Testudines:* Turtles
3. *Squamata:* Snakes, Lizards and Amphisbaenians
4. *Rynchocephalia:* The Tuatara

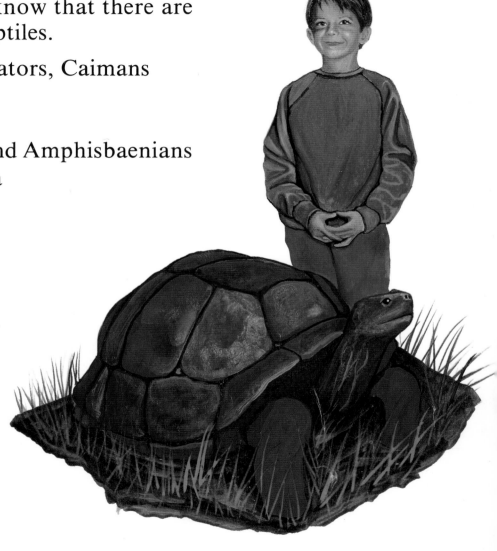